B3

TAKE A TIN CAN

Other books by the same author

TAKE A TIN CAN

How to make decorative models

Richard Slade

Faber & Faber
3 Queen Square, London

First published in 1973
by Faber and Faber Limited
3 Queen Square London WC1
Filmset and printed in Great Britain
by BAS Printers Limited Wallop Hampshire
All rights reserved

ISBN 0 571 09834 7

Contents

Photographs

Introduction

What we generally call tin is really tinplate. This consists of a thin sheet of mild steel coated with pure tin.

This invention made an equally clever invention possible, namely, the tin can, by which means food, drink and other goods may be preserved and safely dispatched to faraway places.

Tin cans, once they have served their purpose, are usually thrown away. But we can still put them to some use.

Tin has a silvery sheen pleasant to look at, and we can make attractive models from it.

For example, take a tin can . . . . . .

1. Materials

Quite a number of useful articles can be made from tin. In books about metalcraft you will find instructions how to make flour scoops, candlesticks, ash trays, picture frames and many other items of use around the house, all from tin. The aim of this book is to show you how to make articles from tin which are decorative rather than useful. It is also meant to furnish you with ideas for creating work of your own design.

Our most handy and cheapest form of tin is the tin can. Tin may, of course, be bought in sheets from a sheet-metal supplier; but with a little extra trouble we

can provide ourselves with all the tin we shall need at practically no cost.

Perhaps the most common type of tin can is that used for soups, vegetables and fruit. These are found in most homes.

Another type of tin easily come by is shown in Photograph 1. These oil tins are the best sort of tins for our models, especially the quart size. Line a cardboard box with newspaper and ask a grown-up to get some for you from the local petrol station: these places use a lot of them and the empty cans are put in the dustbin. The gallon size are harder to obtain, since empty ones are kept for waste oil and other purposes.

The manager at a supermarket will sometimes let you have large tins. They are used for tongue, ham and other meat sold at the meat counter, and once the meat is removed the tin is thrown away.

Beer and soft drink cans made of aluminium may be used, but are not recommended. They do not have the texture of tin, nor can they be polished to the lustre we wish to achieve on some of our models. They are very difficult to solder.

Since tin cans are plentiful, choose only those which can easily be cleaned and are suitable for the purpose you have in mind. You might make a collection of cans and experiment with them to find those you prefer. Practice in cutting is all to the good and should not be neglected.

Wire

Various kinds of wire may be used with tin. Soft, pliable wire of various thicknesses is sold in coils in tool shops and ironmongers'. Steel piano wire of different gauges can be bought in handicraft and hobby shops.

The soft wire is easily cut with pliers which have a cutting edge.

Remember that the steel piano wire should be divided with a file.

Use a file also to point wire which has to be pushed into a wooden base.

Beads
Beads are most easily obtainable in the form of necklaces. Imitation pearls go well with tin work. Ask around your grown-up relatives. You will probably find someone with old strings of beads which are no longer wanted.

Other materials are:

Wood for bases
Glass marbles for eyes
Sandpaper, wood stain and varnish for bases
Fine emery paper
Finest quality steel wool
Thinner
Lacquer
Enamel paints
Small wooden balls
Core solder
Soft rivets

2. Tools

Tin snips or shears

These are for cutting the tin. There are different sizes and types for different jobs, and the type which will do most jobs well is called a straight snips. These will cut straight edges and outside curves without trouble; inside curves take a little extra care. The type used for inside curves is called a curved snips.

When using the snips, remember to close them only partly as you cut: to close them completely will give a jagged edge.

Pliers

The type needed is a small pair of combination pliers. These are a general purpose pliers which have a cutting edge. They are used for cutting and twisting wire and bending metal.

Another useful type is the round-nose pliers. These can be used for coiling wire and curving metal.

Ball pein hammer

This has one end flat and the other rounded. Use a small size. The rounded or ball end is for embossing the tin. (See p. 25).

Soldering iron

A small electric soldering iron of good quality is recommended. This is a useful tool to have around the house for many jobs apart from tin work. A recognised make will last longer and be safer.

A small copper iron which has to be heated at some form of fire can be used instead of an electric iron.

Tin opener

The type shown in Photograph 2 is best for cutting below the rims of cans.

Vice

A small metal-worker's vice which can be clamped to a table. When clamping tin in this put the tin between two

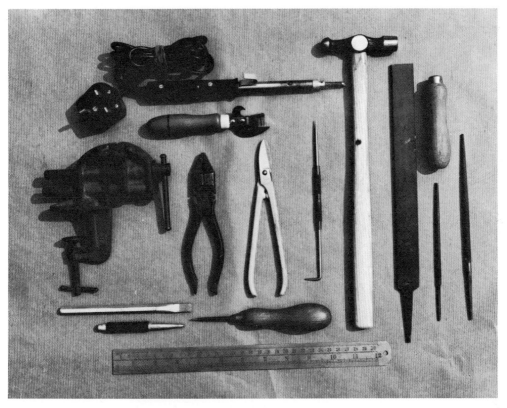

pieces of wood so as not to mark the tin with the jaws of the vice.

Scriber   An engineer's scriber is not expensive. This is for tracing the design on the tin.

Centre punch   Used with the hammer for marking places to be drilled or bored. It can also be used for decorating the tin.

Steel rule   For drawing straight lines on metal. It should have millimetre and centimetre measurements.

Cold chisel   For making slots in metal, and for cutting out small areas where a snips cannot be used.

Awl   For boring holes. If possible obtain a cane worker's awl.
                 This is the type of awl in Photograph 2 and is a most
                 useful tool for the tin worker.

Files   Three kinds of file are needed, a flat, a round and a
                 three square (triangular) file. They can all be small,
                 and should be the smooth type.
                     Handles for these are purchased separately.
                     These tools are shown in Photograph 2.

                 There are many other tools used in metalwork but
                 those mentioned are quite sufficient for all the models
                 in this book.

Homemade equipment

An old kitchen table will do for a bench. The work is
light and there is no heavy hammering to do. The
vice can be clamped to this when needed.

Anvil   A suitable piece of steel or iron must be placed beneath
                 the tin when you use the cold chisel, punch, or do riveting.
                 A very serviceable anvil can be made from the bottom
                 of an old electric iron. This consists of a steel plate. It is
                 removed from the iron and sunk into a bed of wood:
                 trace the shape on a block of soft wood and gouge out
                 sufficient of the wood to allow the plate to be held firmly.

Flat surface   When working with tin it is helpful to have one or two
                 different surfaces handy on which to work. For example,
                 a wad of newspaper will prevent the tin shifting when
                 you are tracing; a block of wood is useful for resting the
                 tin on when filing a corner; when boring holes do so on a
                 block of soft wood: this allows the awl to go through
                 the tin and sink into the wood.

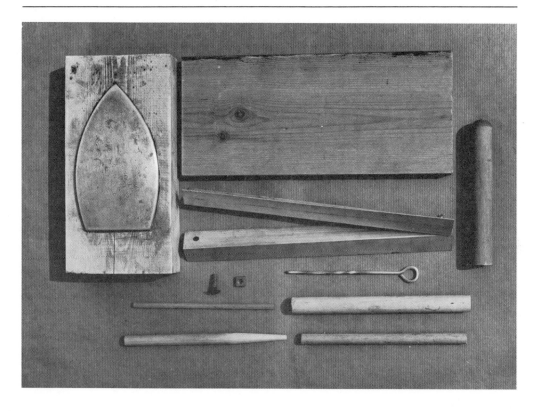

Dowel

Different thicknesses of dowel are very useful when curving tin by hand. They can be clamped in the vice and used for curving tin with the hammer.

Scriber

A home-made scriber can be any hard metal point, such as a dart or meat skewer. The point should be very sharp. Much care must be taken when using a scriber not to scratch the tin unnecessarily. Mark only those lines which are to serve as a guide for the snips or other cutting tool. It will not be possible to remove unwanted scratches.

Folding bars

These are for bending and folding tin. Two pieces of hardwood clamped in a vice so that their edges are level will do. But a better idea is to make folding bars from two pieces of aluminium angle strip, as in Photograph 3.

Bore holes at each end of the strip to take nuts and bolts. The bars are placed in the vice; the tin to be bent goes between the strips and the vice is tightened. The tin can be bent down by hand at first; then place a piece of wood over and tap it with a hammer to finish the bend.

3. Methods

Removing the tin from the can

Photograph 4 shows how the working tin is removed from the can. Use a can opener of the type shown. Push this into the can just below the rim in front of the seam—where the tin is joined along its length. Cut round the can keeping close to the rim until you reach the seam again. The seam will be difficult to cut: to save the sharpness of your snips, work the loose piece backwards and forwards with your hand and it will soon break off.

If you are using an oil can it should now be stood to allow any oil which may be in it to drain out. Put a thick

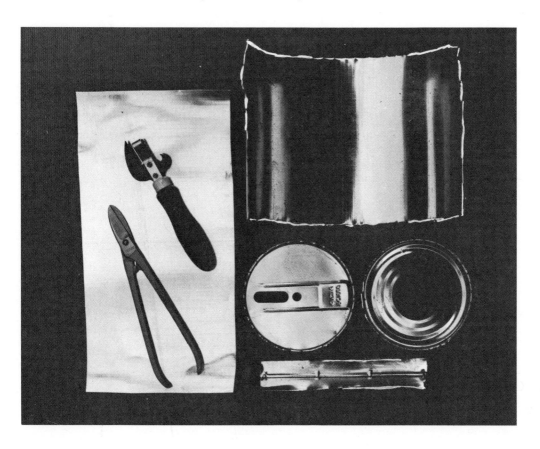

wad of newspaper in a cardboard box and let it drain on this overnight or longer. Do a few tins at a time and you can then prepare a number of working surfaces.

After draining, the can is cut in the same manner beneath the other rim.

The seam is removed with the snips: cut as closely as possible to the seam.

You now have a curved piece of tin with rough edges. Flatten this out by hand: place some newspaper on the bench and gently ease the tin into a flat shape. Be careful not to buckle the tin. When the tin is more or less flat remove the rough edges with the tin snips. This is the tin for your models. If it is greasy clean it with waste rag and thinner, or wash it in hot soapy water and wipe it dry.

Oil tins will have the outside painted. To remove the paint first take off the gloss by rubbing it over with steel wool; then rub it well with the wool dipped in thinner. The paint comes off fairly easily this way. Finish by wiping the tin with a dry rag and polishing with dry steel wool. It is best to clean the tin this way before beginning a model as you then have a choice of surfaces: one surface may be better than the other.

Drawing the design on the tin

The method of drawing the design on the tin used throughout this book is as follows:

(a) Draw the design on paper. This has been done for you in the full-size diagrams for each model.

(b) Place tracing paper—greaseproof paper will do—over the design, keeping it in position with a couple of paper-clips, and trace the design with a pencil.

(c) Turn the tracing over and shade the back of the traced lines with pencil.

(d) Clip the tracing, right side up, on some thin, light-coloured card and go over the tracing with a biro or hard pencil, pressing down firmly.

This will transfer the design to the card.

(e) Cut out the design from the card and use it as a template. Place the template on the tin and go round it with a scriber. Instead of a scriber you can use a fibre pen or a soft pencil: these will mark the tin clearly but rub off easily.

The preparation of these templates does mean more work but it is an excellent way of drawing designs on tin. Also the templates may be used more than once: write what they are on the templates and keep them together in a large envelope.

Cutting the tin shape

When the design has been drawn on the tin, cut away as much of the unwanted tin as possible without actually cutting the design, as this will make the cutting-out easier. Unwanted tin may be useful later, so have a box in which to keep scraps of cut tin.

Straight snips will do most of the cutting, including curves. Curved snips are not essential, but if you find this sort of work interests you, you should get a pair. Leave the snips slightly open at the end of each cut to prevent jagged edges.

Filing

Cut edges should be filed to render them less sharp. For straight edges use a flat file; for inside curves, a round file; and for corners a three square file. File in one direction only: push the file away from you.

Alternatively fine emery paper can be used on the edges. Wrap this around a small wooden block and you won't damage the sides of the tin.

Joining tin

Three methods of joining tin are used here.

(a) Tab and slot: a tab is left on the tin shape which is to be joined to another shape. A slot to receive the tab is made with a cold chisel in this other shape. The tab is pushed into the slot and bent over to secure it.

Some shapes need more than one tab and slot. Make the slot smaller than required and gradually widen it to fit the tab neatly. This method of joining is used for the dragonflies, as will be seen from the photograph. This method can often be substituted for soldering, but remember to leave tabs when you cut out shapes.

(b) Riveting: use a small size of soft rivet. Bore holes in each piece to be joined slightly smaller than the diameter of the rivet and enlarge these so that the rivet fits neatly through the holes, that is without the tin shifting about. If the rivet is too long a piece can be snipped off with the pliers or removed with a file: enough must be left for hammering down and securing the tin. Place the head of the rivet on the anvil and tap the shank gently with a hammer until it has been flattened out and the tin joined securely.

(c) Soldering: the type of soldering used here is called soft soldering. This is the easiest form of soldering.

The surfaces to be joined must be perfectly clean. Use fine steel wool for this.

Solder must be used with a flux to make it flow. You should buy a cored solder. This looks like wire and has a core of flux already in it.

The tip of the soldering iron must also be clean. It can be filed lightly to clean it. Before the iron is used the tip is tinned, that is given a thin coating of solder and allowed to cool.

If you are using a soldering iron which has to be heated in a flame, it is ready for use when the flame turns green—do not overheat it. An electric iron is ready as soon as it will melt the solder easily.

Hold the iron against the surface of the tin where the join is to be made, to heat the metal first, then feed the solder to the tip of the iron, moving the iron slowly as the solder melts. Practise this on scraps of unwanted tin until you get the knack.

Sellotape will keep pieces of tin in place for soldering.

Boring holes in tin

Holes are made with an awl or similar sharp point.
You can make holes larger with the point of a round file. Push the point through the hole and twist it round. A piece of hard dowel pointed at one end will do instead of a file. The tin will project a jagged edge on one side of the hole and this should be filed away, but do not scratch the surface of the tin with the file.

Embossing

To emboss metal means to raise a series of little bumps on it for decorative effect. Place the tin on a piece of soft wood and tap the area you wish to emboss with the ball part of the ball pein hammer. Keep the embossing close and as evenly spaced as possible. Practise on some scraps of tin first to get the idea and learn how hard you should hit the tin.

Polishing, lacquering and painting

Polish the tin with very fine steel wool. When the model is finished give it a coat of clear lacquer put on with a soft brush and this will keep it bright.
Tin work may also be painted, the pattern for painting being drawn on the shape with a fibre pen or soft pencil. Enamel paint is recommended.

4.   Models

FISH ORNAMENT

photograph 5
plate 1

1. Trace the shape and make a template from card.
2. Trace around the template on tin.
3. Cut out the tin shape.
4. Make holes for the eyes.
5. Smooth all cut edges with a file.
6. Make small holes for decoration in body with an awl or nail point.
7. Make a wooden base and insert three lengths of wire bent in a wavy line in this.
8. Solder fish shapes to the wire. Or they can be neatly fastened at the back with Sellotape.
9. Lacquer.

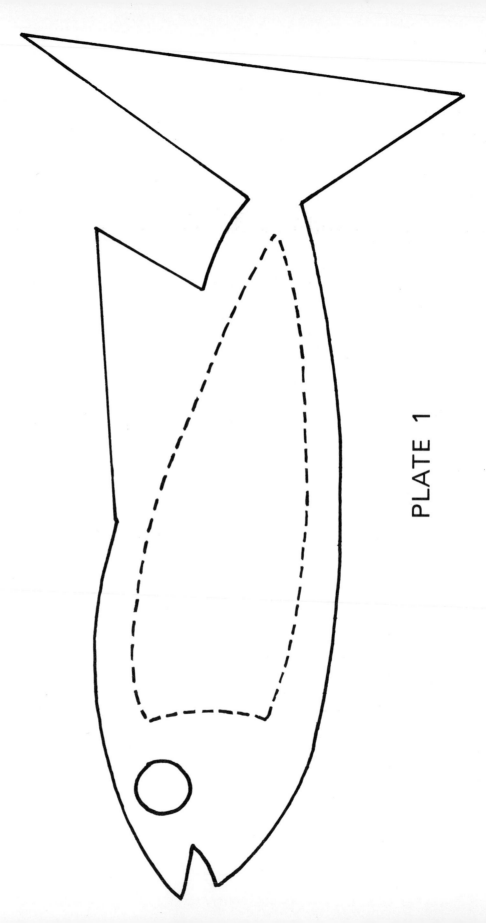

PLATE 1

FISH ORNAMENT

photograph 6
plate 2

1. Cut template; trace and cut fish shape as in fig. 1; bore hole for eye. A small bright bead may be inserted here.
2. Cut five pieces of strong, pliable wire of different lengths and curl at top as in fig. 2. Sharpen bottom of wire with file.
3. Insert wires into wooden base. Drill small holes for wires if necessary.
4. Emboss body of fish, leaving head plain.
5. Curve fish to go round wires.
6. Lacquer or paint.

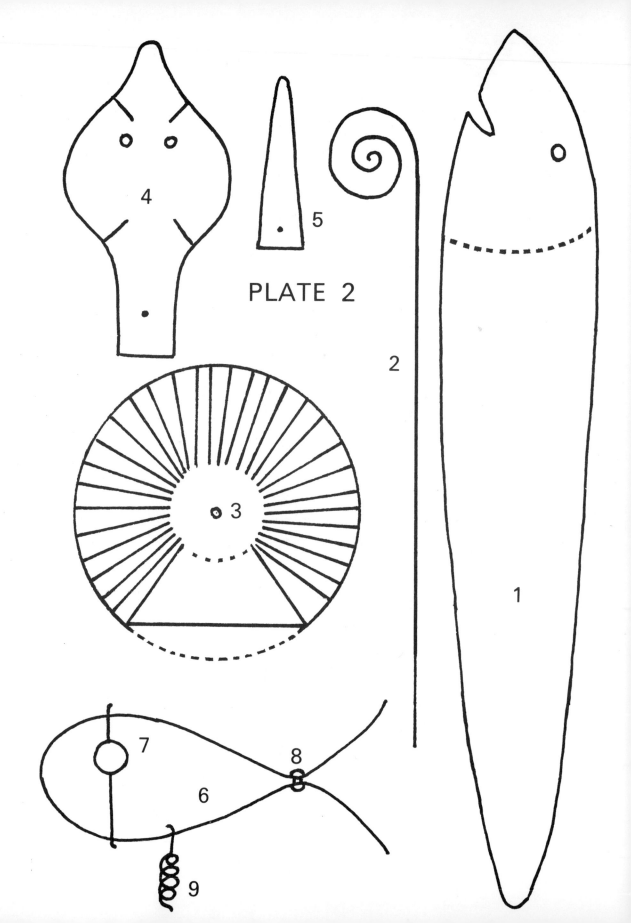

PLATE 2

SWIMMING FISH

photograph 7
plate 2

1. Measure and cut seven strips of tin 29 cm long by 1 cm wide.
2. Smooth edges with file. Take one strip at a time. Bend into fish shape and pierce holes for rivets where the tail begins, fig. 8. The shape and size of the fish can be altered by altering the size of the tail and the size of the body.
3. Rivet the tail. If the rivet is too long take off a piece before hammering it home.
4. Pierce three holes in the body: one at the bottom to take the coiled wire, fig. 9, and two, one above the other, for the 'eye' wire, fig. 7.
5. Cut a short length of thin wire and thread a large bead on it for the eye. If the bead does not fit tightly make a kink in the wire to hold it.
6. Wind another length of thin wire around a pencil to make a coil, leaving one end uncoiled to be fastened to the fish and the other end uncoiled to go into a wooden stand.
7. Make a stand from heavy wood and bore small holes in this for the wires.
8. Lacquer or paint the model.

The wires should be sufficiently thin to allow the fish to move in a breeze.

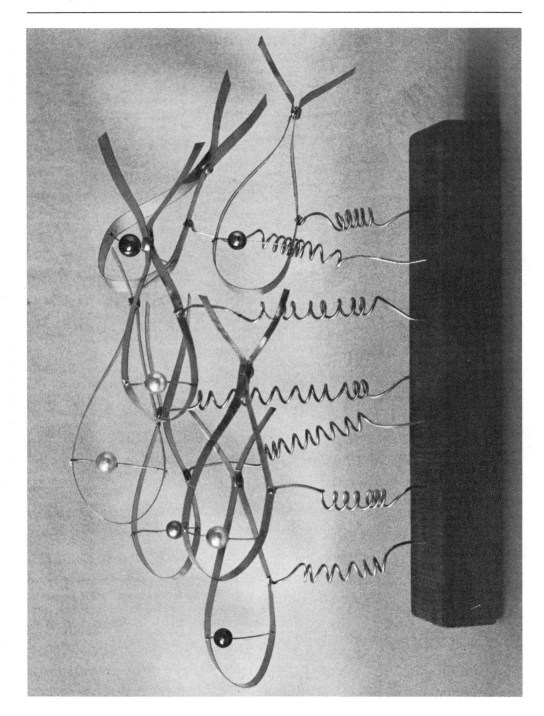

c

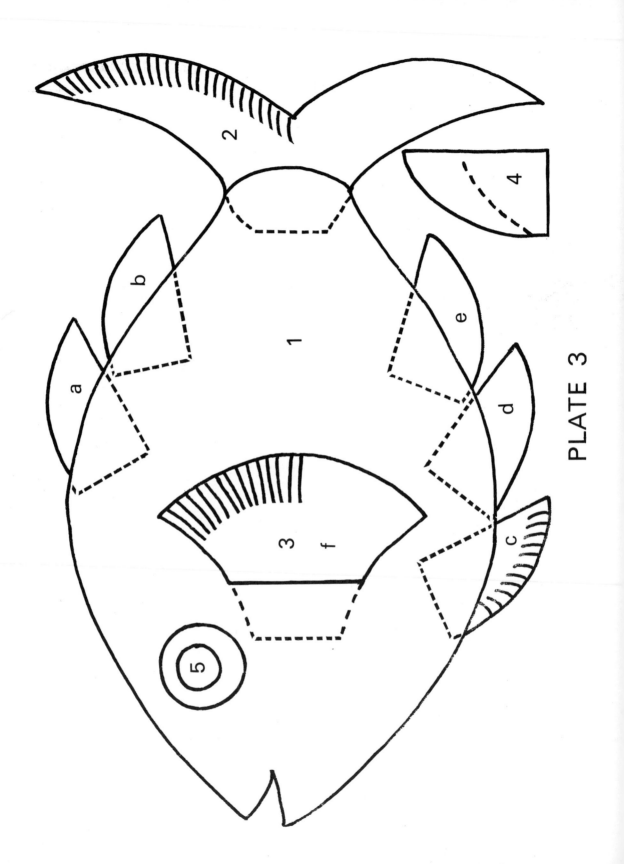

PLATE 3

FISH MOBILE

photograph 8
plate 3

1. Trace and make templates of body, fins and tail, figs. 1, 2, 3 and 4.
2. Draw and cut two body shapes, five fins fig. 4, and two fins fig. 3.
3. Make holes for eyes in fish shapes, fig. 5. These holes must be in the same position in each shape. The eye is a glass marble: check at this stage that it will fit tightly when the two shapes are brought together.
4. Emboss each fish shape leaving a plain margin around the edges, as in the photograph. Fringe the tail and fins.
5. Cut slots for the side fins as at f.
6. The tail and fins can be soldered or riveted in place. The side fins must be fixed before the fish is put together. Leave fins a and c until last: insert marble eye before fixing these.
7. Lacquer.

A single fish can be made and used as a mobile as in the photograph, a circle of wire being firmly secured in a piece of hard, heavy wood. Or three or more can be hung as a mobile from a piece of dowel.

HEDGEHOG

photograph 9
plate 2

1. Cut four tin circles 8 cm in diameter, as in fig. 3. Cut two tin circles $7\frac{1}{2}$ cm in diameter, and four $6\frac{1}{2}$ cm in diameter.
2. Remove segment from each circle, and fringe as at fig. 3. Carry fringe as far as the small circle.
3. Cut and make head (fig. 4). This shape is formed as in the photograph. Two small, bright beads are fitted into the eye holes: a spot of lacquer will act as glue. Cut a tailpiece (fig. 5).
4. Holes of the same size are pierced in the centre of each circle piece, and at the points shown on the head and tail shapes (figs. 4 and 5). Bend all fringes slightly to give a bristle effect.
5. Each shape is now threaded on a short thin piece of dowel through the hole in each. The dowel must fit tightly. The four large circles go in the centre; each side of this come the two circles next in size; and the four remaining circles are placed two on each side of these. Lastly the head and tail are put on the dowel.
6. Lacquer.

CATERPILLAR

photograph 10
plate 4

1. Cut 14 tin circles and remove a segment from each as in fig. 1.
2. Cut around this to make a fringe, as in fig. 2. Make a card template the size of the inside circle, fig. 2, and trace round this with a fibre pen or soft pencil on each shape before cutting to act as a guide for the depth of the cut. Make a small hole in each shape where shown.
3. Cut shape as in fig. 3. Fringe this.
4. Thread all these shapes on a length of strong twine. A single bead at each end will keep the whole secure; four beads are placed on the twine between each shape (fig. 8a). The small fringed shape, fig. 3, is put at the tail end. There must be no slack twine.
5. Cut the head shape, fig. 5. Make the head by bending a over b under c and riveting these ends in position; see the photograph and fig. 8b. Solder head to body with tin strip (fig. 6).
6. Make eyes as in fig. 7. Thread a bright bead on a short piece of thin wire. Loop this wire at one end and solder the loop inside the head so that the eye protrudes a little from the eye socket.
7. Cut and make the tailpiece, fig. 4. Curve the shape and put a over b to form a shallow cone (fig. 8c). Solder this to the tailpiece, fig. 3.
8. Lacquer.

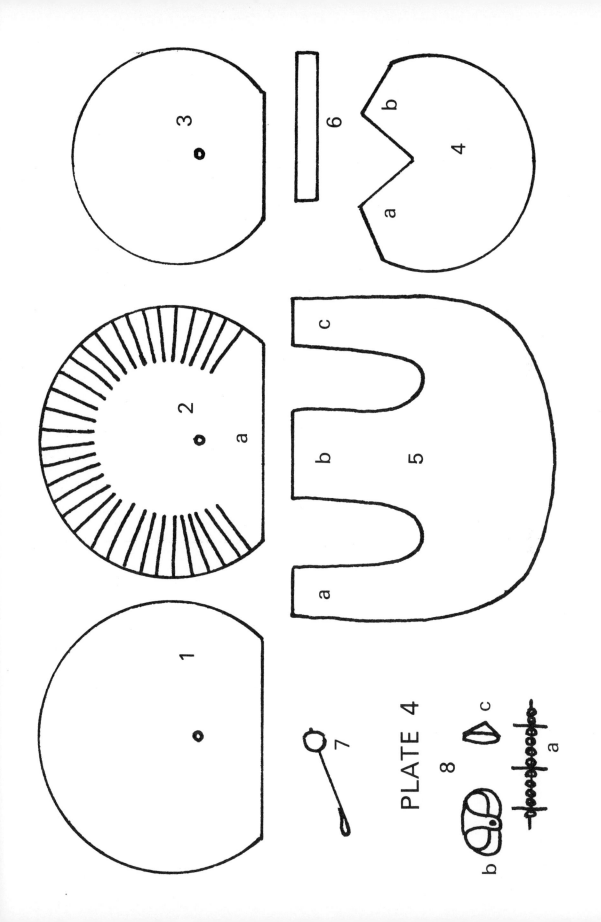

PLATE 4

FLOWERS

photograph 11
plate 5

1. For each flower cut two shapes as in fig. 1. Solder or rivet one shape on the other and curve the petals, top shape upwards and bottom shape downwards.
2. To make the stems cut some long, narrow strips of tin. Twist these into a spiral by curling them round a piece of thin dowel or something similar. One end is soldered beneath the flower and the other is cut to a point and inserted into the wooden base.
3. Cut two or more leaf shapes (fig. 2). Give these a wavy curve. Cut a point at the bottom to put in the base.
4. Make a wooden base and have as many slots in this as necessary to take the stems and leaves.
5. Lacquer.

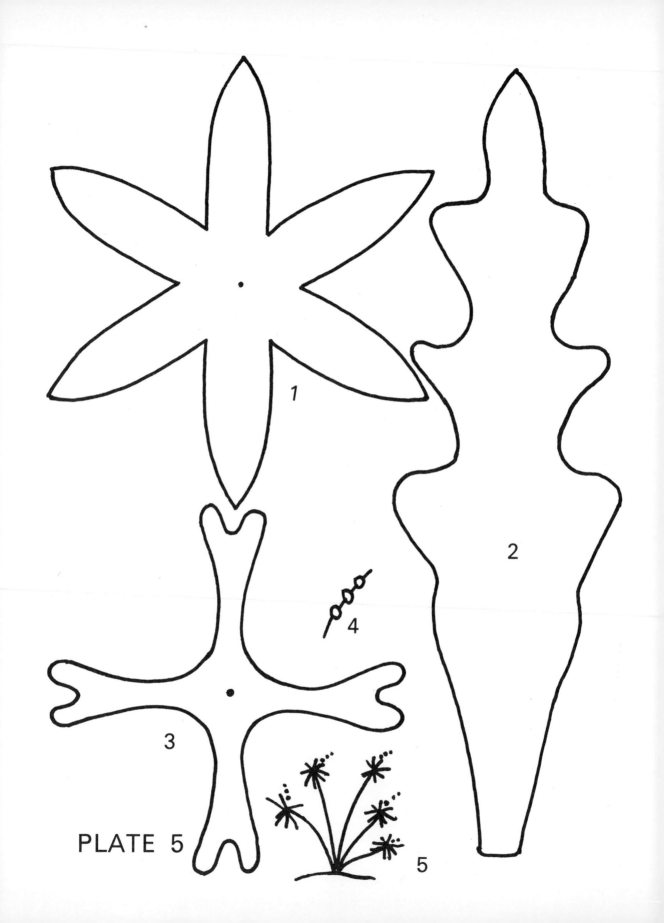

1

2

3

4

PLATE 5

5

FLOWERS

photograph 12
plate 5

1. For each flower cut two shapes and pierce at centre (fig. 3).
2. Cut as many pieces of piano wire (cut with a file) as needed of different lengths for the stems. Sharpen bottom ends with a file.
3. Use small wooden balls if obtainable (otherwise large beads), drill these and push wire through to give a tight fit (fig. 4).
4. Place flower shapes on top of wooden ball and thread some beads on top of these.
5. Insert the stems in a wooden base (fig. 5). Lacquer or paint. If you paint the flowers, do this before assembling.

LILIES

photograph 13
plate 6

1. Cut one petal (fig. 1), for each flower and roll this to form a cone shape: see photograph. Bend the tip slightly at the top.
2. Solder each flower to a length of piano wire, leaving part of the wire protruding above the flower and decorate this with a bead or beads (fig. 2).
3. Cut leaves (fig. 3), and point the ends for insertion in the base. Curl the leaves slightly.
4. Arrange flowers and leaves on a wooden base, making the necessary holes in the base for the wire and slits for the leaves (fig. 4).
5. Lacquer.

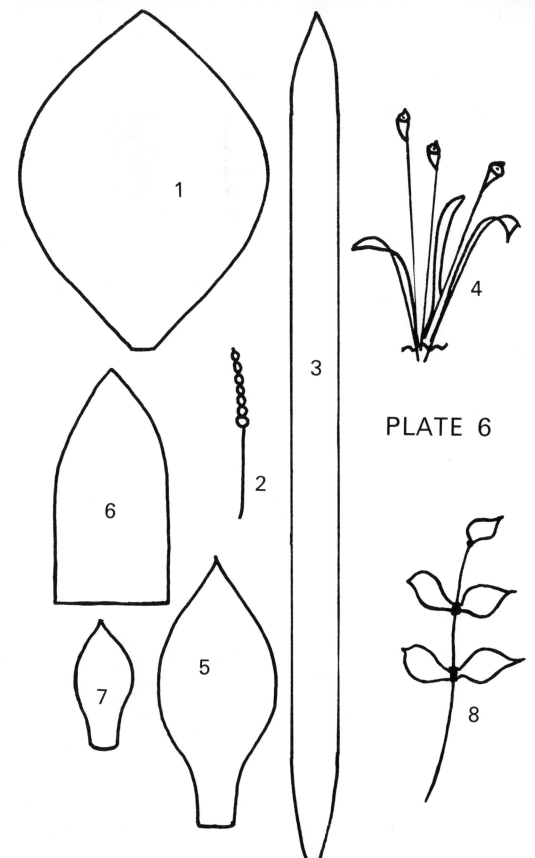

1

3

4

PLATE 6

2

6

7

5

8

D

ROSES

photograph 14
plate 6

1. Cut petal shape (fig. 6), and roll it round a piece of thin dowel to get shape for rose centre.
2. Cut four petal shapes (fig. 5), and curve round dowel for outside petals.
3. Assemble centre and petals in the shape of a rose and solder the bottom of the flower on to a length of strong pliable wire. Use plenty of solder and shape this to form a calyx.
4. Cut leaves (fig. 7), and solder these on pliable wire (fig. 8).
5. Sharpen ends of wire with file and insert in a wooden base.
6. Paint the whole with gold metallic paint. It helps to put an undercoat on first: mix some red oil colour with white undercoat for this.

BUTTERFLIES

photograph 15
plate 7

1. Cut each wing separately as shown at the side of the butterfly in the diagram. The body is made from a short piece of soft dowel, or shaped from balsa wood. Assemble the butterflies by pushing the wings into the dowel: if the tabs for this are too long, adjust by cutting them. Remove and re-assemble after painting.
2. Draw pattern wings with a fibre pen or soft pencil. Use enamel paints. Use thin pliable wire for antennae.
3. Cut several lengths of thin piano wire. Some of these are pushed into the bodies of the butterflies, some into short lengths of dowel to give a bulrush effect: see photograph.
4. Insert all wire in a wooden base. A slight breeze will give movement.

PLATE 7

DRAGONFLIES

1. Cut four wings (fig. 1).
2. Cut body (fig. 2), and make four slots (shown by the dotted lines) before curving, for the wing tabs. Curve on a piece of dowel to get the body shape: see photograph.
3. Insert wings with bottom pair overlapping top pair. Bend tabs inside body to secure.
4. Cut two lengths of pliable wire and shape as in figs. 3 and 4. Solder these to inside of body, fig. 3 at head and fig. 4 at tail end: see photograph.
5. Lacquer.

A few of these make an interesting decoration on a wall.

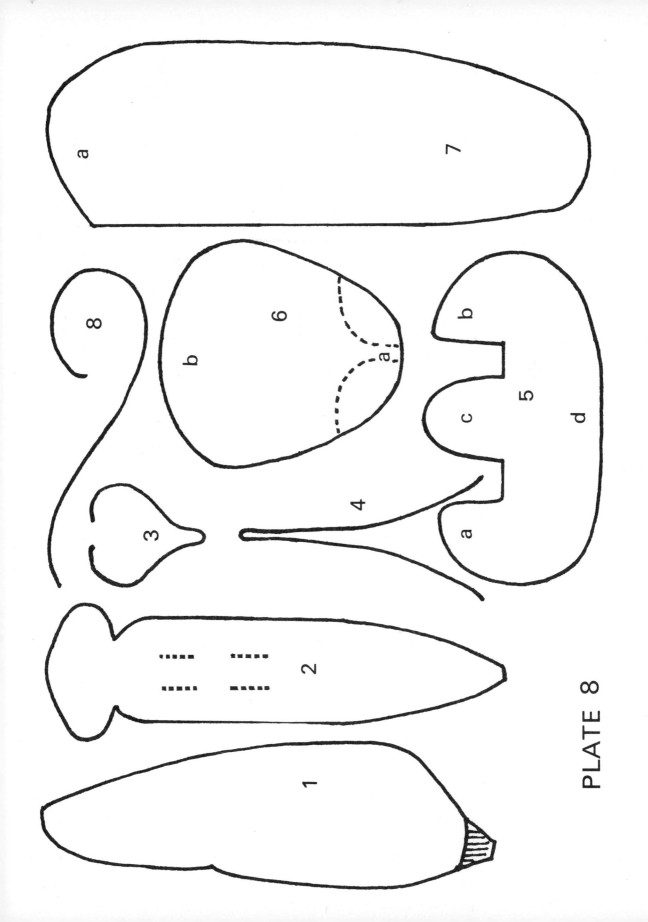

PLATE 8

BEETLE

1. Cut two body shapes (fig. 7), one body shape (fig. 6), and one head shape (fig. 5).
2. Solder two body shapes—fig. 7a shows the top—to the other body shape at the dotted lines (fig. 6a). All the shapes should be slightly curved before soldering.
3. Curve the headpiece so that a and b meet under c: these are not joined. Solder this beneath body at fig. 6b and fig. 5d.
4. Cut two lengths of pliable wire, shape as in fig. 8 and solder ends to inside head: see photograph.
6. Cut six legs and solder in position beneath front of body. If small loops are made in the wire they will assist the soldering.
7. Lacquer.

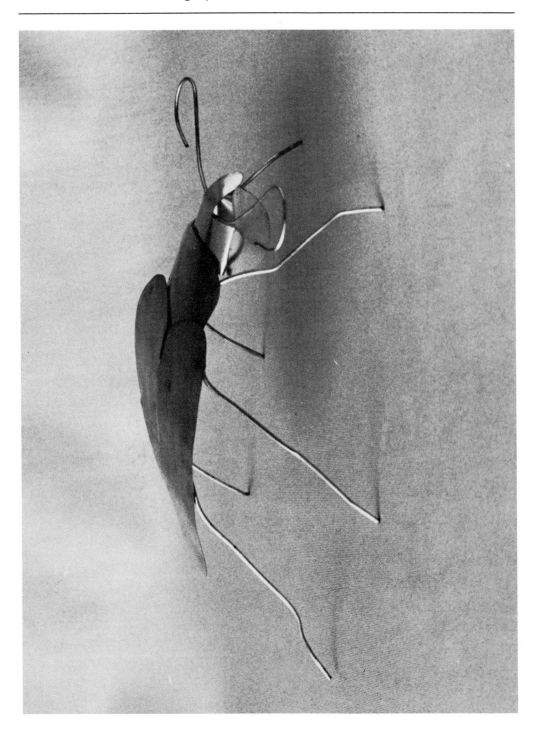

STABILE

photograph 18
plate 9

1. Cut two shapes as in fig. 1. Curve these into a shallow S shape.
2. Cut a small piece of tin as in fig. 2, and roll round a thin knitting needle to make fig. 3. Solder this to the centre of each fig. 1 shape.
3. Cut a length of piano wire long enough to take both shapes and beads as in the photograph, and thin enough to let the shapes spin freely. Mount this wire in a wooden base.
4. Thread on beads at intervals, below, above and between the shapes.
5. Lacquer.

The shapes should turn in a light breeze.

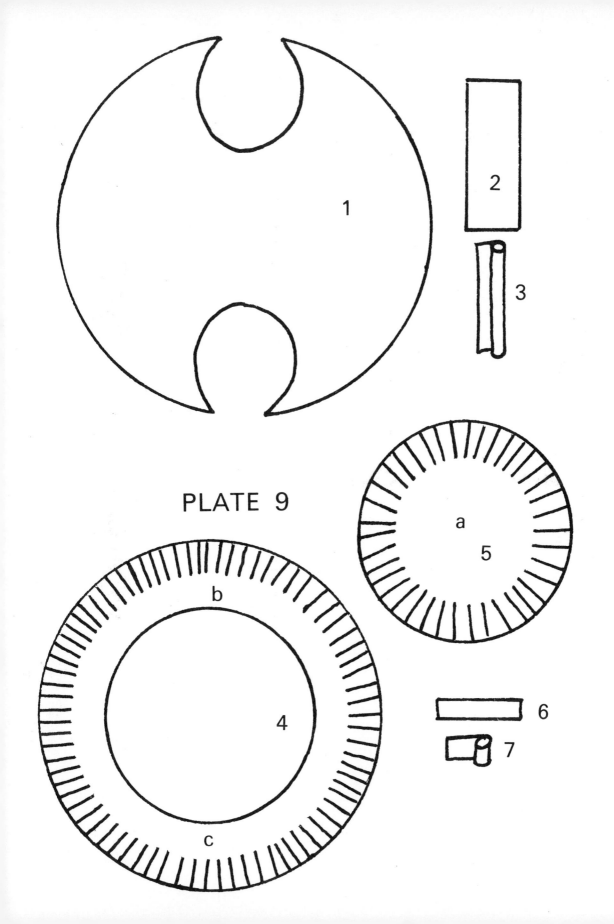

PLATE 9

STABILE

photograph 19
plate 9

1. Cut three circles of tin, remove the centres and cut fringe (fig. 4).
2. Cut three circles and cut fringe (fig. 5).
3. Bend all fringes singly in alternate directions: see photograph.
4. Cut nine thin strips of tin (fig. 6), and shape each as in fig. 7.
5. Solder these shapes (fig. 7), to centre of small shapes (fig. 5a), and to bottom and top of large shapes (fig. 4b and c).
6. Insert a length of piano wire in a wooden base and thread the shapes on the wire as in the photograph, using beads as spacers and to keep the shapes in position. The beads should fit tightly and the shapes swing freely.
7. Lacquer.

The three decorative figures which follow are based on ancient American pendants made from gold. Paint the tin figures with gold paint. It is best first to give the tin an undercoat, red oil colour mixed with white undercoat. The finished figures can be mounted on board covered with red or purple velvet or similar material. This will make an attractive wall hanging.

PENDANT

photograph 20
plate 10

1. The finished model is shown as fig. 6 and is made from the other shapes.
2. Cut one of each shape: figs. 1, 2, 3, 4 and 5.
3. Cut nose with a cold chisel (see photograph); pierce holes for the eyes and mouth. Alternatively these features can be made as in the diagram by indenting the tin.
4. Make dents around the circle with the centre punch and solder it to the body piece (fig. 5a).
5. Solder headpiece, fig. 2, to the head. Solder arms to back of body at shoulders.
6. Paint and mount as described above.

PLATE 10

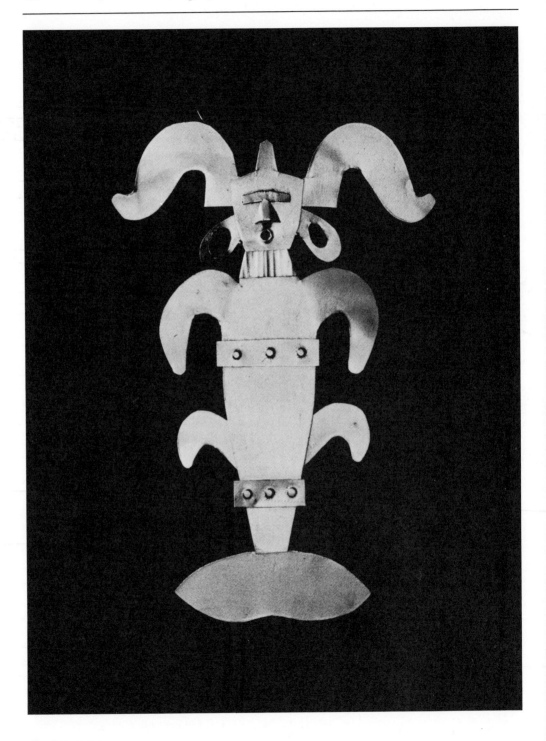

PENDANT

photograph 21
plate 11

1. Cut shape, which includes head, fig. 1.
2. Cut one shape each, figs. 2 and 6. Cut two shapes each, figs. 3, 4 and 5.
3. Cut three strips of tin, as shown in the photograph: two pieces to be riveted on the body, and one piece for the collar. The collar piece is made large enough to clip behind the neck at each side: it is decorated with marked lines made with a cold chisel.
4. Make hole for mouth and fix the nose piece by slotting in shaded tabs.
5. Solder shapes 2, 3, 4, 5 and 6 to back of figure.
6. Rivet decorative strips in position.
7. Paint and mount as described above.

PLATE 11

PENDANT

photograph 22
plate 12

1. Cut shape, fig. 1, which includes head.
2. Cut shapes, fig. 2 (two) and fig. 3.
3. The eyes and nose can be made in one or two ways. The nose shape (fig. 4), and two shapes for eyes (fig. 5), can be cut out and fixed to a piece of tin (fig. 6). Or, as in the photograph, a strip of tin is riveted to the head and a small amount of metal drilled away from the rivets to make the eyes. The nose is made by leaving a triangular shape on the tin strip when you cut it, and bending this over.
4. Holes are made below the neck and rivets form a necklace for decoration.
5. Solder ear pieces at back of head.
6. Solder some thin strips of tin at back of mouth for teeth; slot or solder mouth in position.
7. Paint and mount as described above.

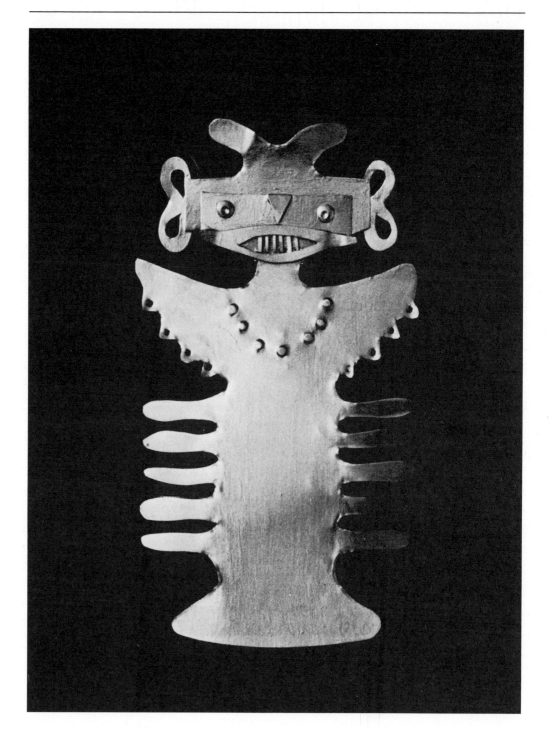

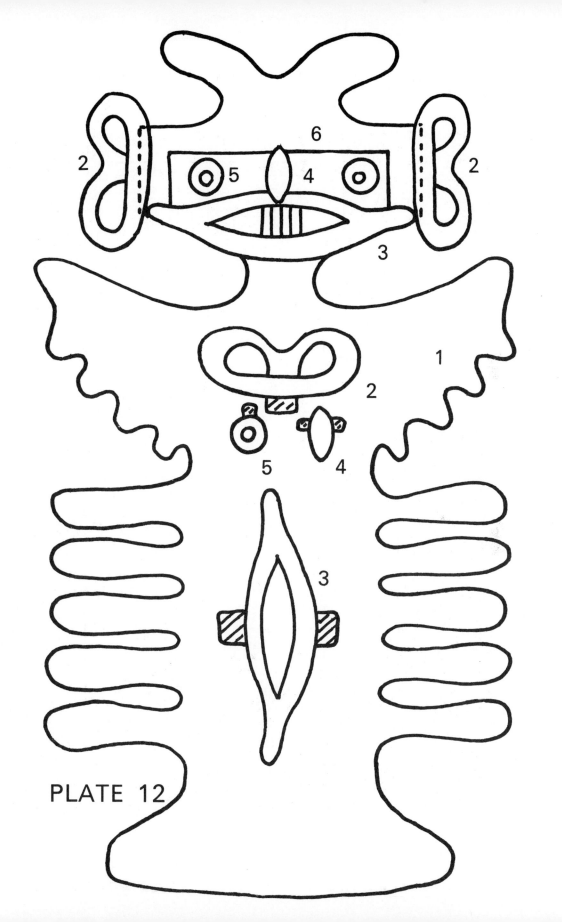

PLATE 12

The following are based on a Polynesian mask, an African mask, another Polynesian mask and a Mexican mask, in that order.

MASK

photograph 23
plates 13 and 14

1. Cut three shapes, figs. 1, 2 and 3. (Plate 14).
2. Make the eyeholes in shape fig. 1 just large enough to hold a large bead or glass marble securely in place. Obtain the beads or marbles before cutting the holes.
3. Paint the shapes before assembling, but first curl the nose piece at the bottom and make a slot in shape 1 for fixing the tab, fig. 3a.
4. Assemble by soldering shape 1 to shape 2 at back and fixing nose with tab and slot join.

PLATE 13

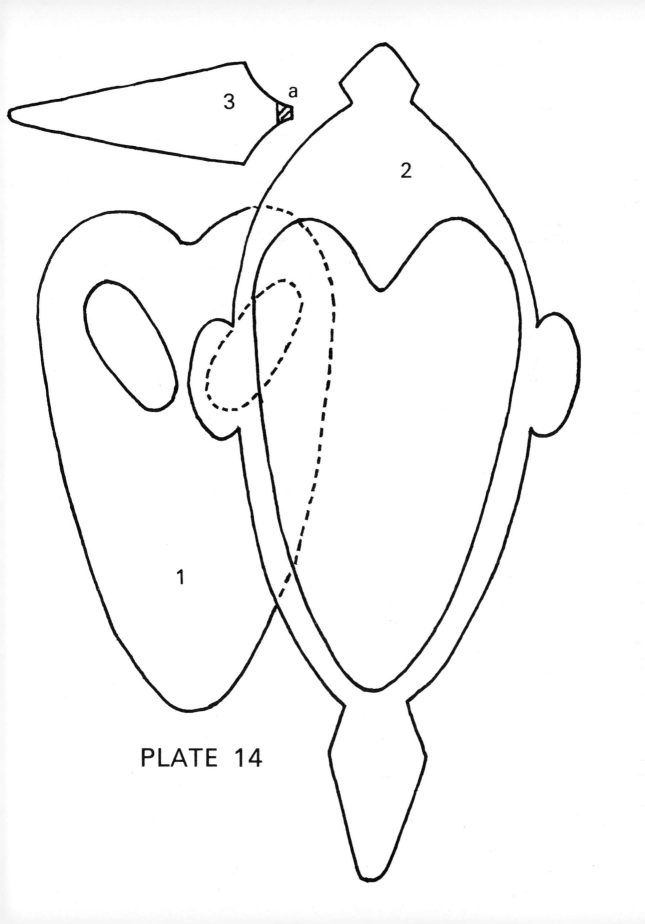

PLATE 14

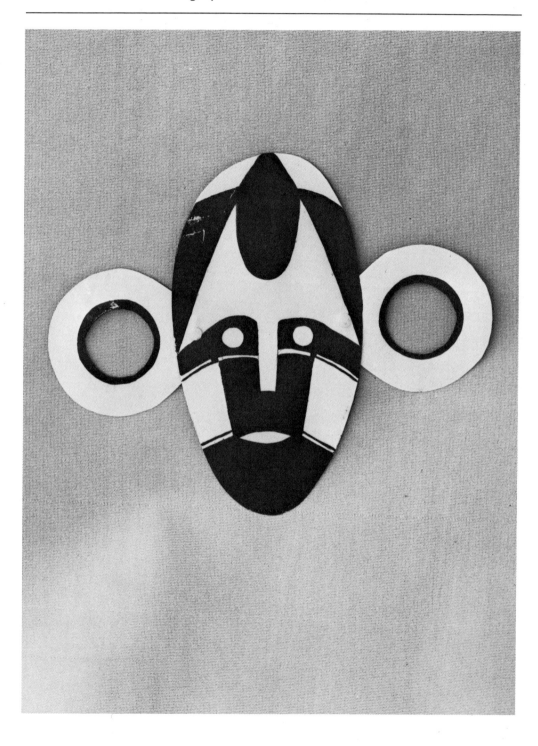

MASK

photograph 24
plates 15 and 16

        1. Cut shape as in Plate 15; trace design and paint.

        2. Cut two shapes as in fig. 6 Plate 16 and paint.

        3. Rivet or solder ear pieces to head.

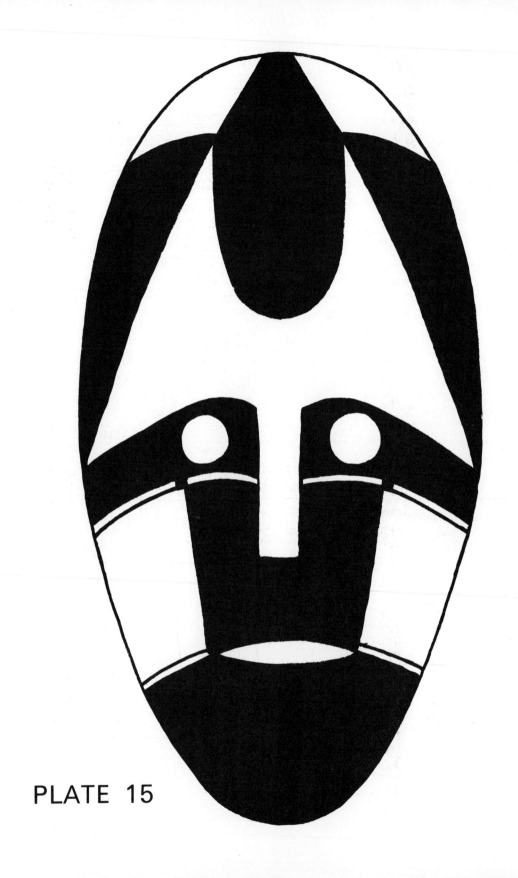

PLATE 15

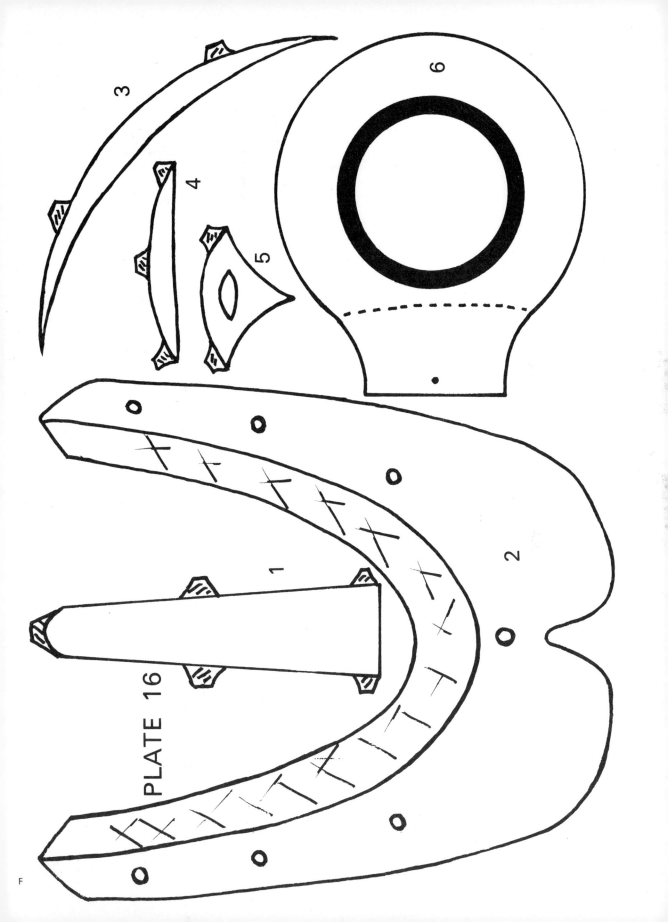

PLATE 16

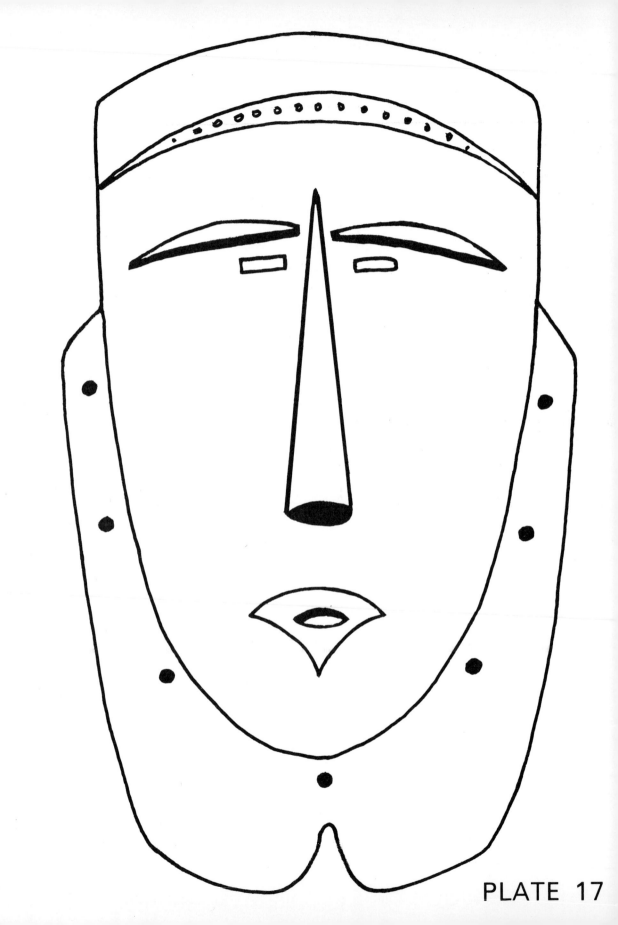

PLATE 17

MASK

photograph 25
plates 16 and 17

1. Cut main head shape (Plate 17), and make holes in this for eyes.
2. With the ball pein hammer emboss the chin and sides of face. Rest the tin on a piece of soft wood and tap with the rounded end of the hammer so that the tin curves inwards to give a rounded shape; and finally curve the top of the head by hand.
3. Cut shape as in fig. 2 Plate 16, and put rivets round it for decoration. Solder this shape to the head.
4. Cut two eyebrow pieces (fig. 4, Plate 16); nose piece (fig. 1) and mouth piece (fig. 5). These can be joined by the tab and slot method or soldered. If they are to be soldered, omit the tabs. The same applies to shape fig. 3.
5. Cut decorative head piece (fig. 3), pierce holes in it and join to forehead.
6. Lacquer or paint.

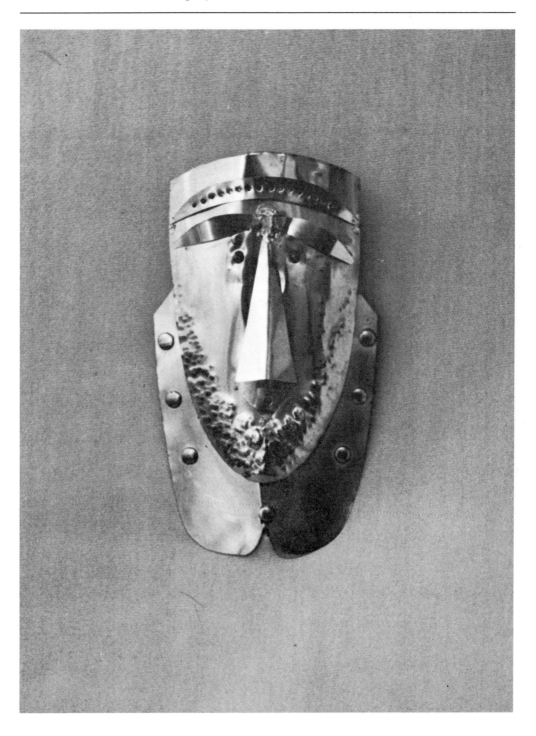

MASK

photograph 26
plates 18 and 19

1. Cut head shape, (Plate 18 fig. 1). Make holes for eyes and mouth. These can be cut with a cold chisel and filed smooth. Curve the chin and part of the face (to the dotted line) by embossing with the ball pein hammer. Curve rest of shape by hand.
2. Cut head piece (Plate 19 fig. 1), and draw line with fibre pen around the edges of this as a guide line for the decorative holes. Pierce small holes along the line.
3. Cut circle piece (Plate 19 fig. 2). Pierce holes around this and emboss; fix this to centre of head piece with a rivet.
4. Rivet head piece to top of head.
5. Cut nose piece (Plate 18 fig. 3), and rivet a and b to c to make the nose. Solder nose to head, so that solder will be hidden by the eyelashes.
6. Make and fix eyelashes (Plates 18 and 19 figs. 5). Cut four shapes and fringe them. The tabs are soldered at the back of the eyeholes.
7. Cut two ear pieces (Plate 18 fig. 6). Pierce holes round the edges. Solder to back of head.
8. Cut two teeth shapes, (Plate 18 fig. 4). Solder behind mouth hole.
9. Make the lips. Cut two pieces each (figs. 3 and 4 Plate 19). This is the most difficult part of the mask to make. Shape 3 is curved and shape 4 is soldered to it. The photograph will show what is meant. The lips protrude from the mouth. Solder the two finished lip shapes to the mouth on the inside.
10. Cut four shapes (Plate 19 fig. 6), for ear ornaments. Join two shapes to make one ornament and rivet them in the centre. Hang from the ears with thin wire.

11. The eyes are made with large imitation pearls and thin pliable wire. Thread the wire through the pearl and secure it. Then coil the wire a few times and make a loop at the end (fig. 2 Plate 18). Solder the loop to the back of the head just below the eyehole.

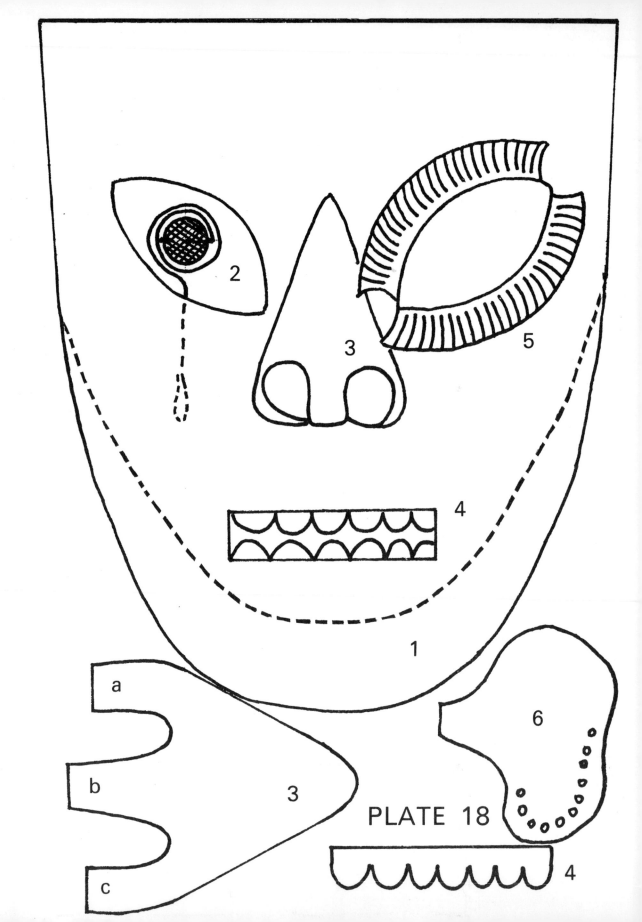

PLATE 18

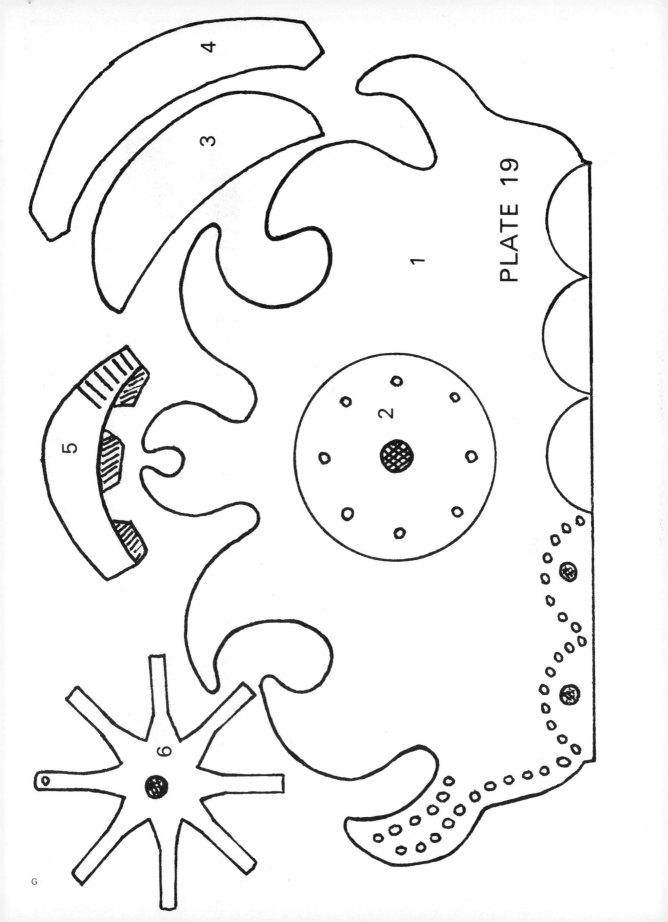

PLATE 19

When you have had some practice at making models out of tin, you may wish to try something more difficult. A medieval ship will make an interesting model. The Victoria and Albert Museum in London has a fine collection of nefs, models of ancient ships sometimes made of precious metals and used for a special purpose. The museum also publishes a book called *Medieval Silver Nefs* by Charles Oman, which is worth studying for ideas.

NEF

photographs 27 and 28 plates 20, 21, 22, 23 and 24

plate 20

Fig. 1 This shows the curve of the keel.

Fig. 2 This gives the width of the keel piece. This is bent and flattened. The dotted lines show where it is bent and fig. 3 shows how it is bent, the final shape being quite flat. Since the length is too long to be shown to scale the diagram is broken and the measurement given beneath. When the keel piece has been cut and folded flat, curve it to shape, as in fig. 1, with the V cuts at a on the inside.

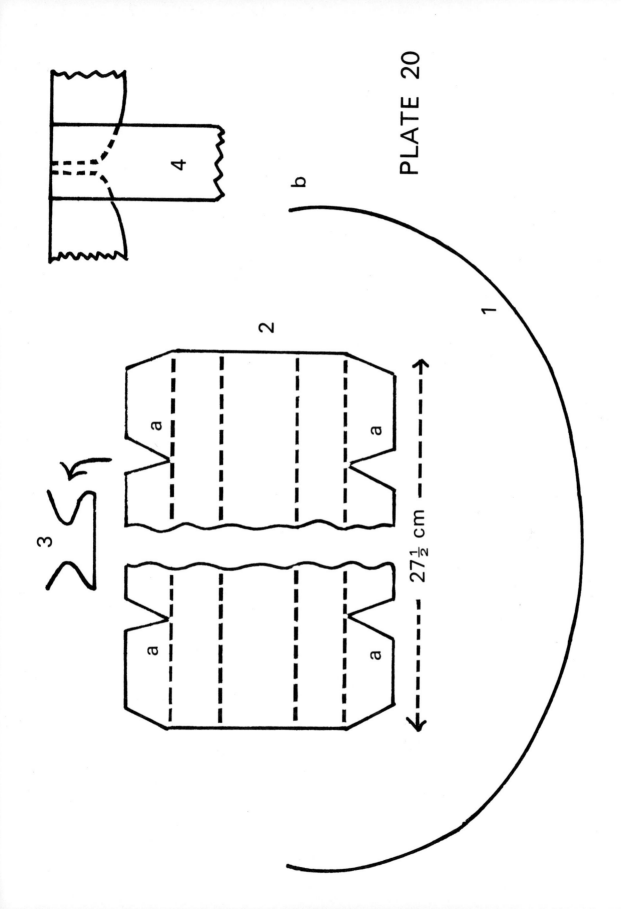

PLATE 20

plate 21

Figs. 1, 2, 3, 4 and 5 Cut two each of these shapes and assemble in the order shown, shape one being at the top. The method of assembly is shown on Plate 20 fig. 4, and can be seen in the photographs. Each piece is pushed into the slot made by folding the keel piece. Insert shape 2 beneath shape 1 so that shape 1 overlaps it and so on. These are soldered in position on the inside; but first assemble the sides to get them right, then take them apart and solder back into place one at a time. A spot of solder where the strips meet the keel should be enough. One side can be soldered first.

Figs. 6 and 7 These are the pennant shapes, which can be cut later. Cut two of 6, one for the foremast and one for the mizzen. Roll the shaded portion to fit the flagpole as at fig. 8.

plate 22

Fig. 2 This shows the bottom piece of the hull. Cut two of these with small tabs. These pieces are curved slightly and should fit into the bottom of the keel. The tab is soldered against the bottom side piece on the inside.

Fig. 1 This is the deck piece. Cut one of these from tin and one from stiff cardboard. Make mast holes in both pieces. The cardboard piece acts as a stiffener and as a support for the ends of the masts. It is placed inside the hull as deeply as it will go. The tin deck piece is soldered in just below the top of the hull. Do not solder the deck in position until you have made the masts and are certain that they will fit into the mast holes securely and without forcing.

Figs. 3 and 4 give the shapes for the crow's-nests. Fig. 3 is for the mainmast and fig. 4 for the foremast. First cut out circles of tin and draw circles on these to mark the limit of the V cuts. The cut edges are turned up to make the crow's-nest. Make the holes for the masts before cutting the edges. They should fit tightly: the holes in the diagram do not give the exact size as it will depend on the size of your masts.

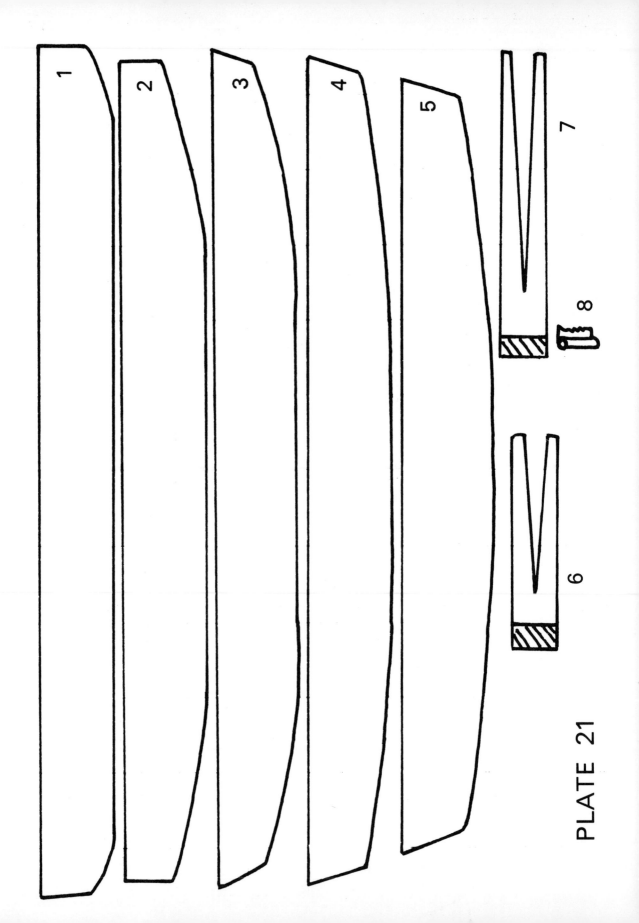

PLATE 21

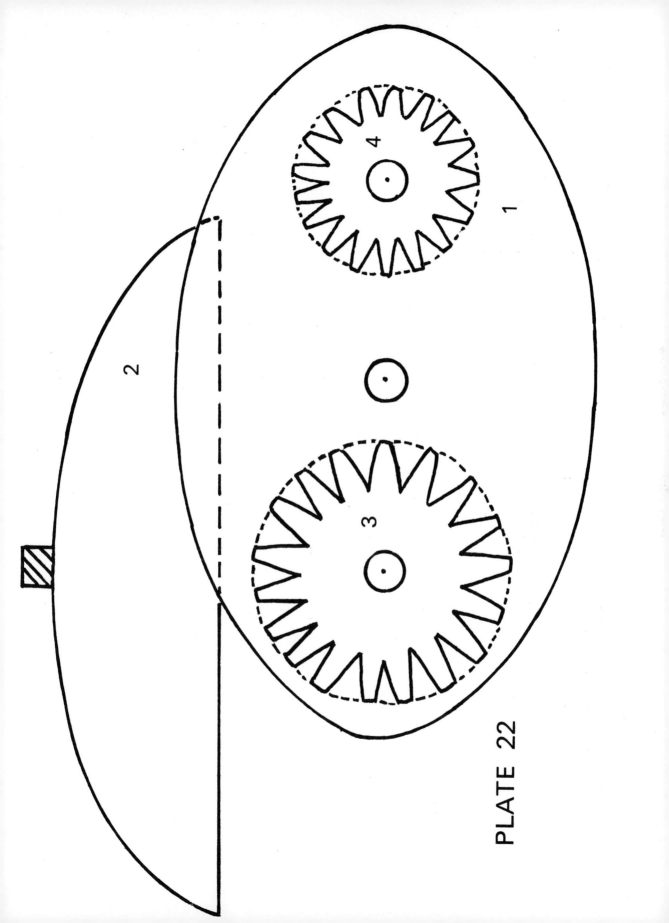

PLATE 22

plate 23

Fig. 1 This is the shape for the stern- and fore-castles. Trace the shapes with a scriber but before cutting them out cut away the rectangular windows with a cold chisel and trim them with a file. The shape can then be cut out. The castle is made by bending the shape at the dotted lines: a meets b and is soldered on the inside. A hole to take the mast is made in each shape and the shape is soldered to the deck after the mast holes have been checked. Each castle must protrude a little from the hull.

Fig. 2 This is the shape for making the masts. The length is too long to be shown to scale, so the drawing is broken and the measurement given at the side. The shape is tapered so that when it is rolled the top will be smaller than the bottom. To start rolling the mast bend one edge in the folding bar. With a suitable length of thin hard dowel or better still a thin iron rod, shape the fold into a curve and proceed from there: place the fold on a hard surface and hammer the dowel or rod into it. The finished mast shape should be something like fig. 3. The top of the mast is closed with solder. When the masts are in position the mainmast should be the tallest and the foremast and mizzen about the same height. Fit the pennants (Plate 21 figs. 6 and 7) on short lengths of piano wire and solder them to the top of the masts. The bowsprit is made like the masts but somewhat smaller. It is soldered to the forecastle by means of a tab left on when the shape is cut out.

Fig. 4 gives the shape for the shrouds. Make two of these from pliable wire. The cross pieces, called ratlines, are from thinner wire and are wound on the shroud wire at intervals as at fig. 5. The loops are tightened to hold the wire in place.

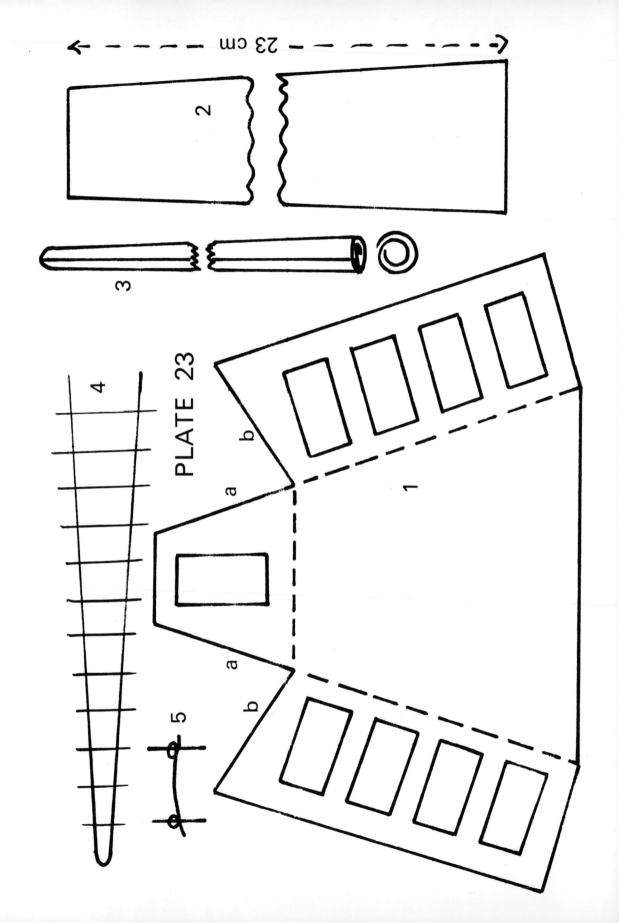

PLATE 23

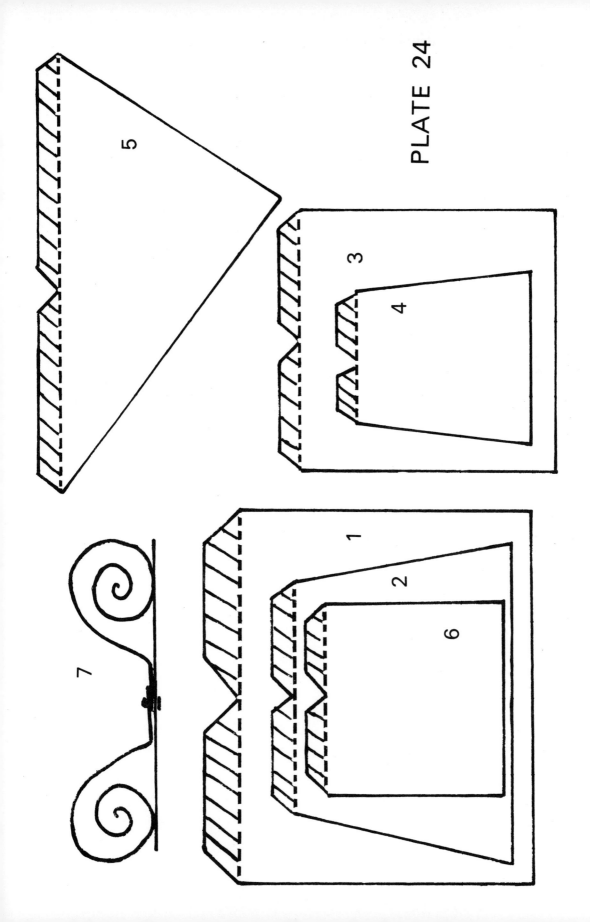

PLATE 24

plate 24

Figs. 1, 2, 3, 4, 5 and 6 are the shapes of the sails. Cut one of each. The shaded portion is folded over a length of piano wire as in the photograph. Curve the sails. Fix them to the mast with a short piece of thin pliable wire bent double: this is fitted over the piano wire at the V cuts, and the double ends are then opened out, put round the mast and twisted together. Figs. 1 and 2 are for the mainmast; figs. 3 and 4 for the foremast; fig. 6 the bowsprit sail; and fig. 5 the lateen sail for the mizzen mast. A stay wire is stretched from the bowsprit round the masts to the stern castle.

Fig. 7 This is a side view of the stand. Cut four strips of tin about 28 cm long and 7 mm wide, and a rectangle of tin about 10 cm by 7 cm. Each strip is rolled as shown and two strips are riveted one on top of the other on each long side of the rectangular piece: see diagram and photograph. This can be put on a wooden base or left as it is.

When completed the model is lacquered.

5.   Sources of Supply

Large tins may be obtained from garages and super-markets. It is best to ask a grown-up to get these for you. Pliable wire of different gauges is sold in coils at most tool shops and ironmongers'.

Piano wire is usually sold in handicraft and hobby shops where balsa wood is also sold. These shops will have soft dowel in stock.

Glass marbles can be obtained in small bags at Woolworths.

Beads are best bought as necklaces.

The snips shown in the illustrations were supplied by the Gilbow Tool and Steel Company of Sheffield; they are called jeweller's shears and are very suitable for making models from tin. Most good tool shops carry Gilbow products or will obtain them for you. Ask for Jeweller's Shears No. 56, 7 inch Straight Blade. The curved type are No. 056, 7 inch Bent Blade.

Joy Clear Lacquer and Joy Metallic Paints can be recommended and are found in most hardware stores and paint shops.

Belco Thinner sold by Halfords is very good.

Golden Fleece Steel Wool is a very fine steel wool used largely for domestic purposes, and will be found in stores selling domestic supplies. It may be bought in packets containing a few pads or in a roll.

Multicore solder can be obtained from tool shops and ironmongers'.

Humbrol Enamel is a good quality sold in hobby shops.